Sand Play!

Super SANDsational Ideas

By
Terry Taylor

Dover Publications, Inc.
Mineola, New York

Introduction

What's great about sculpting sand? Everything! Easy molding, easy cleanup, use it over and over again, what a great invention! It is like having fun at the beach in your home! I turned my sculpting skills to this new medium and came up with fun projects for you and your family to create and enjoy together. Keep your camera handy to photograph your works of art!

I have spent many years developing craft projects and teaching children to sculpt. This book is designed to be easy to use, with easy instructions and lots of pictures of the sculpting sand projects in progress for you to follow. Have fun creating!

Visit my studio online at www.TerryTaylorStudio.com
and see what else I've been up to!

Bibliographical Note
Sand Play! Super SANDsational Ideas is a new work, first published by Dover Publications, Inc., in 2014.

International Standard Book Number
ISBN-13: 978-0-486-79479-2
ISBN-10: 0-486-79479-2

Manufactured in the United States by Courier Corporation
79479202   2014
www.doverpublications.com

Credits: Book design and photography: Terry Taylor Studio. All projects © Terry Taylor Studio 2014.

Project Difficulty

Projects with one star are the easiest to do, and are good starter projects for beginners. Two star projects are a little more difficult, and three star projects are more challenging. Build your sculpting skills with the easier projects then move on to the harder ones.

Bunny &
Carrot

Owl

Cat &
Mouse

Mama
Bird

Frog

Funny
Trio

Dragon

And
More!

Table of Contents

Tools & Supplies

Build your *Sand Play* tool box! Did you know that anything can be a sand tool? The projects in this book were designed to use some recycled materials and a small amount of tools, most of which you may have around your home. Supplies, tools, shape cutters and textured foam sheets are available at craft or art supply stores, and online stores.

Let's get started! You will need wooden chopsticks, straws, wood or plastic sculpting tools, a pencil, paper clips, a recycled office tape roller, wooden craft sticks, toothpicks, a knife, a fork, shape cutters, a recycled bowl, a recycled egg carton, and foam texture sheets. It will also help to have other things to make textures, and different size containers to mold the sculpting sand.

Safety Tip!
Once a tool has been used for sand it is best not to use it for food. Keep it only for sand use.

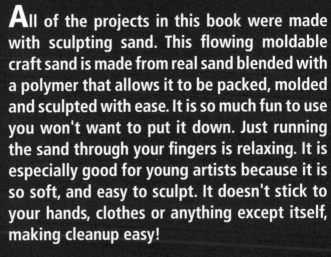

All of the projects in this book were made with sculpting sand. This flowing moldable craft sand is made from real sand blended with a polymer that allows it to be packed, molded and sculpted with ease. It is so much fun to use you won't want to put it down. Just running the sand through your fingers is relaxing. It is especially good for young artists because it is so soft, and easy to sculpt. It doesn't stick to your hands, clothes or anything except itself, making cleanup easy!

Sculpting sand is available from a few different manufacturers and is sold at craft, novelty, and online stores.

Sculpting sand is usually sold in two pound (910g) packages. I recommend that you have four pounds of sand available to use to create the projects in this book.

Techniques & Tips

1. **Molding the Sand:** Tightly pack the sculpting sand into a small bowl or other container; turn the container over to remove the molded sculpting sand.

2. **Packing the Sand:** Tightly pack the sculpting sand together in your hands or against your work surface to form a mound to use for building. The tighter you pack the sculpting sand the easier it will be to make the projects.

3. **Making a Ball:** Roll the sculpting sand in a circular motion in the palm of your hands to form a ball. It works best to use very little pressure while rolling. For smaller eye-sized balls, use a finger tip to roll the ball in the palm of your hand.

4. **Making a Cone Shape:** Make a ball of sculpting sand, place it on your work surface, and roll only one side to form the cone. Your hand should be at an angle to the sand.

Tips

Work Surface: Use a piece of cardboard, foam board, matt board or even construction paper on a hard flat surface. Working on a board or paper will allow your piece not to stick to the table and make turning it easier. When working with children, I have found that a plastic table cloth is helpful to keep the mess under control. It also makes cleanup a breeze.

Lifting and Moving: Use a piece of stiff paper, a craft stick, or a spatula to slip under your coils or cut pieces of sand to help you move them into place on your artwork.

Texture: Sculpting sand is all the same color so adding texture to your piece will add a lot of visual excitement.

Keeping the Sand Clean and Dry: Your crafting sand will last a long time and can be used over and over again if you take the time to keep it clean and stored in a sealed container. If your sculpting sand gets wet, let it air dry before using again.

Working with Sculpting Sand: I have found while working on the projects in this book that humidity and even the heat from my hands really affects the way the sand sticks together. If you find that your projects will not pack and stay together you might want to run your hands under cool water and dry. Then work with the sand again.

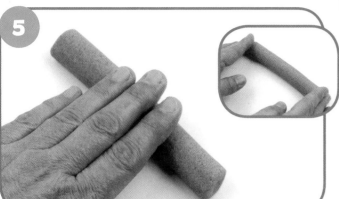

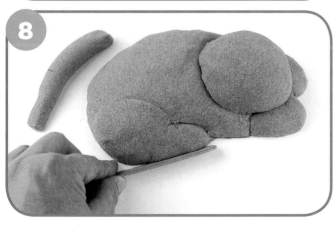

5. **Rolling Coils:** Place the ball of sculpting sand on the table and roll gently back and forth in one direction to form a log shape. Use very gentle pressure; using too much pressure will make the sand come apart. Compress the ends of the coil every few rolls.

6. **Molding Coils:** Use a drinking straw to scoop up the sculpting sand. Tap the sand filled straw on your work surface to pack the sand. To release the coil from the straw, gently roll straw on the table.

7. **Cutting Shapes:** Flatten sculpting sand with the palm of your hand against a hard surface. Use shape cutters or a knife to cut the sand into the shapes you need.

8. **Refining Edges:** Use a craft stick, a knife, or sculpting tools to compress the edges of the sculpting sand and refine your sculpture.

Clown

Difficulty Level: ★

Tools:
Shape Cutters
Chopstick
Toothpick
Texture sheet
Knife

Directions:

1. Flatten a handful of sand and use a circle cutter to make base for clown face. Use small diamond, circle and oval cutters to cut out shapes for facial features.

2. Place an oval of sand in the middle of the circle to make the nose. Use a toothpick to draw a line for the mouth.

3. Add two diamonds of sand for the eyes. Place two small circles of sand at each end of the mouth. Press all pieces gently into place.

4. Use the end of a chopstick to add a pupil to each eye.

5. Flatten a handful of sand with the dotted texture sheet to make a pattern for the hat. Use a knife to cut out a triangle shape.

6. Position triangle on the top of the head and press the corners to fit over the circle.

7. Use some loose sand to add hair; let the sand fall through your fingers to give it a fluffy texture. Use a toothpick to break up any clumps of sand.

8. Add a ball or cut out a flower and add it to the point of the hat.

Clowning Around!
Try making silly or sad clown faces using different shapes.

Funny Trio

Difficulty Level: ★

Directions:

1. Compress and flatten a handful of sand for each face and cut out a square, a circle, and a rectangle with cutters.

2. Add different texture pattern to each shape using texture sheets. A dot pattern, a wavy pattern, and a brick pattern are shown. You can use any pattern to texture the sand that you like. You can also choose not to use textures.

3. Flatten a handful of sand and cut shapes for the eyes. Add the eyes to each face. Use the cutters to create an open mouth for each face.

4. Add a little bit of sand in each open mouth and smooth out using the end of a chopstick. Cut out shapes for noses and place on each face. You can also roll a cone of sand to use it for a nose as shown on the circle face.

5. Add a pupil to each eye by indenting the sand with the end of the chopstick. To make a tongue, roll a small coil of sand and position it in each mouth. Teeth can be made by placing a small coil of sand in the mouth and pressing the toothpick into the space between the teeth.

6. Add a line down the middle of each tongue using a toothpick.

7. Add some eyelashes and eyebrows with a toothpick. For a flat top hairdo add some vertical lines to the top of the head with the toothpick.

8. To add a hat, form a triangle by pinching a flat disk of sand. Place it on the head and add details. Make some fluffy hair by cutting out shapes and adding them around the face.

1

2

3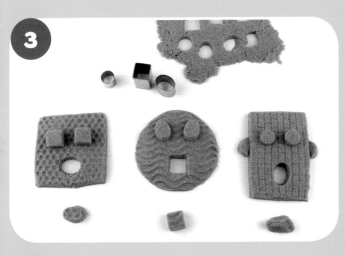

4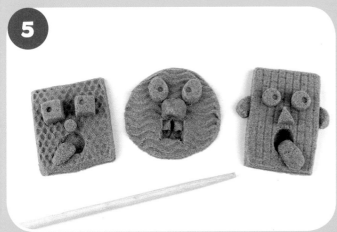

5

6

7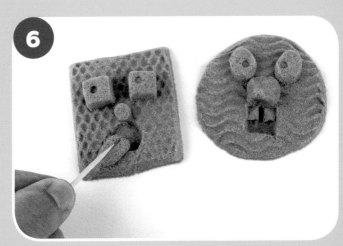

8

Crab

Difficulty Level: ★

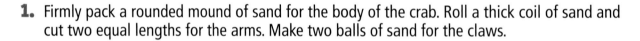

Tools:

Paper clip
Chopstick
Texture sheet
Knife
Craft Stick

Directions:

1. Firmly pack a rounded mound of sand for the body of the crab. Roll a thick coil of sand and cut two equal lengths for the arms. Make two balls of sand for the claws.

2. Press the ends of the coils up against the body and smooth the surface. Press a ball of sand on the end of each coil and smooth. Use a dotted texture sheet to add texture to the crab's body and claws.

3. Cut into the middle of each claw, and open up the space into a v-shape by rocking the knife back and forth. Pinch the end of each claw to form a point.

4. Roll six coils of the same length for the legs of the crab. Position them on the sides of the body. Pinch the end of each coil to form a point.

5. Add lines to each arm and in the opening of the claw by pressing a craft stick into the sand.

6. Use your finger to indent a place for each eyeball. Roll two balls of sand and place one in each indent.

7. Use the rounded end of a paper clip to form the mouth and the eyebrows.

8. Make a pupil in each eye by pressing the end of a chopstick gently into each eyeball.

Leg Tip!
If you are having trouble making the coils for the legs, try packing sand in a large diameter straw.

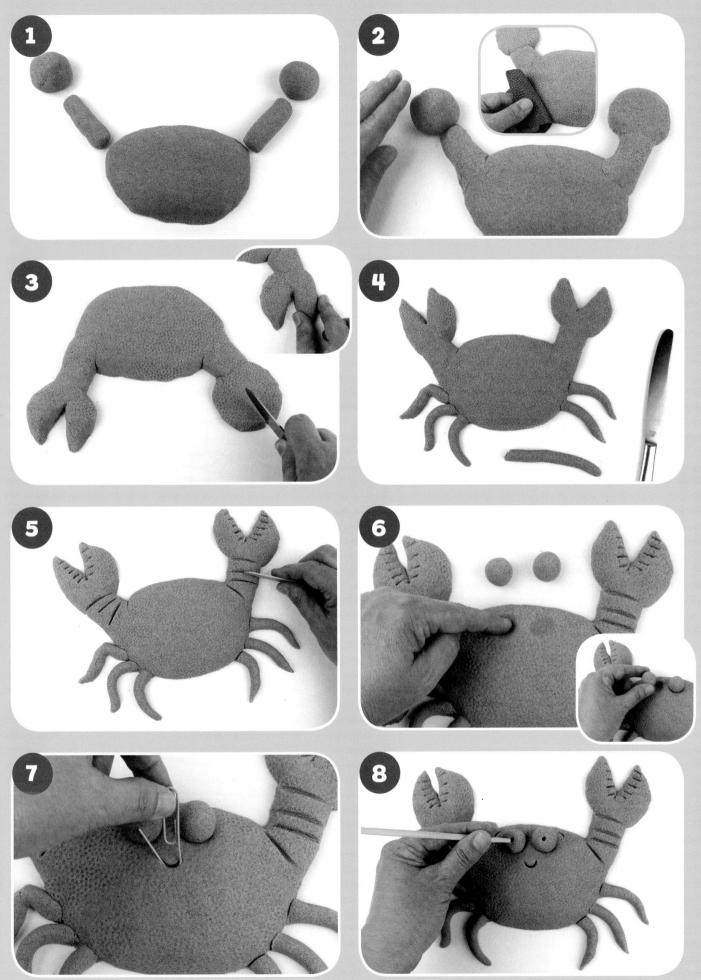

Octopus

Difficulty Level: ★

Tools:

Paper clip
Straw
Chopstick
Craft stick

Directions:

1. Roll eight coils of sand that are tapered to a point on one end. Arrange the coils to look like wavy legs. The legs should be close to the center so that the body of the octopus will cover all the ends. Fill in any cracks in the legs with extra sand and smooth with your fingers or a craft stick.

2. Firmly pack a handful of sand to create the body of the octopus. Position so that all the ends of the eight legs are covered. Adjust the leg positions as needed.

3. Make two indents in the middle of the head using your finger. These indents will hold the eyes in place. Add a smile with the rounded end of the paper clip.

4. Add two balls of sand for the eyes and use the end of a chopstick to create a pupil in each eye. Use the rounded end of a paper clip to add an eyebrow over each eye.

5. Face should look friendly and cute.

6. Use a drinking straw to add circle details to each of the legs. Make the circle marks in a line on one side of each leg.

7. Fill in any cracks with extra sand and smooth with your fingers.

1

2

3

4

5

6

7

Fishy Fun!

Make your octopus an underwater home with a comfy kelp bed!

Maybe you think she needs a few friends. Make her some to keep her smiling!

Lizard

Difficulty Level: ★

Tools:
Pencil
Texture sheet
Paper clip
Sculpting tool

Directions:

1. Roll a tapered coil for the body of the lizard. Roll two coils for the legs and divide each coil in half to make four legs.

2. Add texture to the body of the lizard using the texture sheet. A small dot pattern texture sheet is used for this project.

3. Position the body of the lizard into a wave shape. Fill in any cracks with loose sand and use the texture sheet to compress the sand. Add two legs on each side of the body.

4. To make the toes, slightly flatten the end of each coil. Press the sculpting tool into the end of each foot two times to form the space between the toes. Use the sculpting tool to round off the end of each toe.

5. Add a coil of sand on the back of the lizard and press gently to attach. Pinch the top of the coil into a slight ridge.

6. Press the rounded end of a paper clip into the sand to create the mouth.

7. Make two indents to hold the eyes using the eraser end of a pencil.

8. Roll two balls for the eyes and place one in each of the indents. Add a pupil to each eye using the point of a pencil. Make two nostril holes with the point of a pencil.

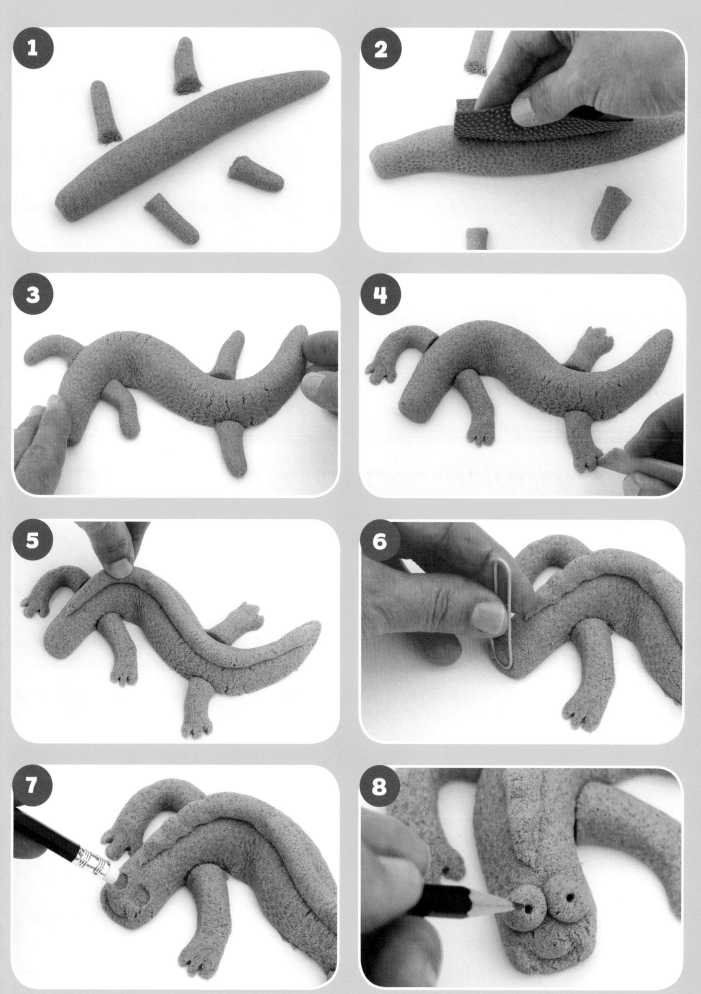

Butterfly

Difficulty Level: ★

Tools:

Shape Cutters
Chopstick
Toothpicks
Paper clip
Tape roller

Directions:

1. Roll four balls of sand and flatten with the palm of your hand. Make two circles for the top wings and two ovals for the bottom wings. Use a craft stick to smooth the edges and top of each shape.

2. Position the circles and ovals as shown. Fill in the opening in the center of the shapes with some loose sand and gently pack the sand into place.

3. Roll a cone shape of sand for the body of the butterfly. Add a ball for the head.

4. Flatten sand and use a shape cutter to create six flowers. Use a tape roller and pack sand into the center to form six circle disks of sand for the wing decorations.

5. Make two indents in the head with your finger to hold the eyes. Roll two eyeballs and place in the indents. Add a mouth by pressing the rounded end of a paper clip into the sand.

6. Use the side of the paper clip to add horizontal lines to the body of the butterfly. Gently press a chopstick into each eyeball to make a pupil.

7. Press the craft stick all along the edge of each wing to add detail lines.

8. Put two toothpicks into the top of the head to make the antennas.

Texture Tip!

Collect buttons and bumpy things to press into the sand. Make a unique texture using found items.

Owl

Difficulty Level: ★ ★

Tools:

Chopstick
Toothpick
Paper clip
Knife

Directions:

1. Make a mound of sand that is firmly packed together for the body of the owl.

2. To form the feet, roll two balls of sand and place them in front of the owl.

3. Take a handful of sand and press it flat on the table. Use a knife to cut out a triangle. Roll two balls of sand for the feathers around the eyes.

4. Press the two balls in place on the face of the owl. Place the triangle on the top of the head and press gently to attach. Use a toothpick to make the detail lines around the eyes and on the edge of the triangle.

5. Roll a coil of sand, and cut two slices for the eyeballs and one for the beak. Center each slice of sand on the previous circles to form the eyes. Press the rounded end of the paper clip into the sand to add feather details to the chest and head. Add three detail lines on each foot with the side of the paper clip.

6. To make the pupils of the eyes use a chopstick to poke two holes in the sand. Use the toothpick to add two nostril holes in the beak.

7. Make two wings shaped like teardrops, with a small handful of sand for each. Position the wings on each side of the owl. Press the wings on both sides of the owl at the same time.

8. Use the paper clip to add feather details to each wing.

Frog

Difficulty Level: ★ ★

Tools:

Chopstick
Toothpick
Sculpting tool
Knife
Shape cutter

Directions:

1. Roll one large, two medium, and two small balls of sand for the frog. Roll a coil of sand for the legs.

2. To form the back legs, position the medium size balls of sand on each side of the large ball and press gently into place. Make two indents with your finger in the top of the large ball. Place the two smaller balls in each of the indents for the eyes.

3. Cut the coil of sand in two equal pieces for the front legs. Position in front of the back legs and press gently to attach.

4. Pack loose sand at the base of each coil to make the front feet. Add sand the same way to form each back foot. Use the knife to pack the edges of the feet and define the shape.

5. Use a sculpting tool or the knife to make four toes on each foot. Press the tool into the sand and gently move it from side to side to form the toes. Round off the front of toes with the edge of the sculpting tool.

6. Use the sculpting tool or the knife to create the open mouth.

7. To make a pupil in each of the eyes use a chopstick to make a hole in the sand. Cut two small circles with a shape cutter from a flattened piece of sand. Then add one small circle of sand to each end of the mouth. Press each circle gently to attach.

8. Use the toothpick to add two nostril holes and to add a curved line to the belly of the frog.

Bunny & Carrot

Difficulty Level: ★ ★

Tools:

Chopstick
Paper clip
Craft stick
Knife

Directions:

1. Firmly pack an oval-shaped mound of sand for the body of the bunny. Roll two short thick coils for the front feet, and roll two longer thick coils for the ears. Make a firmly packed large ball of sand for the head and a small ball for the tail.

2. Position the two coils for the feet at one end of the oval and press gently to attach. Place the head on top of the feet.

3. Place each of the ears at the back of the head, side by side down the back of the bunny. Fill in any gaps or cracks in the sand with loose sand and smooth with a craft stick. Smooth the entire surface of the bunny with the craft stick and your fingers.

4. Make a slit using the knife along the length of each ear. Rock the knife back and forth to form the inside of each ear.

5. Press the rounded end of the paper clip into the lower part of the face two times to form the mouth. Indent two places for the eyes with your finger. Add a ball of sand to each indent to make the eyes. Add a pupil to each eye with the open end of the paper clip. Make two whiskers on each side of the mouth using the side of the paper clip.

6. Add toes to the feet by pressing the end of the paper clip into the sand. Pinch a triangle for the nose and position it on the face, and press gently to attach.

7. Pour some loose sand over the ball for the tail and fluff with the end of the paper clip.

8. Roll a tapered coil of sand for the carrot. Add detail lines to the carrot using the side of the paper clip. Pour some loose sand on the larger end of the carrot to form the carrot leaves.

Mama Bird

Difficulty Level: ★ ★

Tools:

Paper clip
Small bowl
Sculpting tool
Shape cutter
Craft stick

Directions:

1. Tightly pack sand into a small bowl, turn the bowl over to remove the molded sand.

2. Use a sculpting tool or craft stick to make twig texture around the edge of the nest. Add three balls of sand to make the eggs.

3. Firmly pack an oval of sand to form the body of the bird. Using your fingers, make a large indent in one end of the body to hold the head. Roll a ball of sand for the head and place it in the indent. Press gently to attach. Roll a ball of sand for the tail. Make a tapered coil for each wing.

4. Press the tapered coil of sand on each side of the bird to form the wings.

5. Make a small cone of sand for the beak and press it gently on the face. Pinch the end to form a point if needed.

6. To form the tail, add the ball of sand to the end of the bird and pinch the top edge.

7. Using your fingers and a craft stick, smooth all the edges of the wings and the tail. Fill in any cracks with loose sand and smooth it into place. Flatten a piece of sand and use a shape cutter to make two circles for the eyes. Add pupils to the eyes and two nostril holes in the beak with the end of a paper clip. Use the paper clip to make an eyebrow over each of the bird's eyes.

8. Use the rounded end of the paper clip to add a feather texture on the wings and back of the bird. Add lines to the tail using the side of the paper clip.

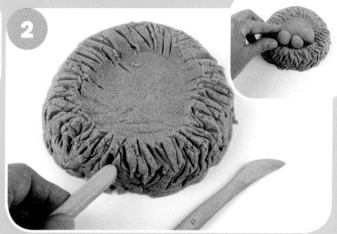

Dog & Bone

Difficulty Level: ★ ★

Tools:
Shape Cutters
Chopstick
Paper clip
Craft stick

Directions:

1. Firmly pack an oval-shaped mound of sand for the body of the dog. Roll three short thick coils for the feet and two thick coils for the ears. Make a firmly packed large oval of sand for the head, and roll a thick tapered coil for the tail.

2. Place the two front feet on one end of the body and smooth into place using your fingers and the craft stick. Add the back leg on the side of the body and pack some loose sand on top of the coil to form the upper part of the back leg. Smooth all cracks and joins with your fingers and a craft stick.

3. Position the head on top of the front legs, and press it gently to attach. Smooth the head with the side of a craft stick.

4. Add the ears on either side of the head, and press gently to attach. Use the craft stick to smooth the surface.

5. Make two indents with your finger to hold the eyeballs. Roll two balls and place them in the indents, and press them gently to attach. Add a pupil to each eye using the end of a chopstick. Make a ball for the nose and press it into position.

6. Use the paper clip to add eyebrows, a mouth, and freckles to the face. Press the paper clip into the end of each foot to form the toes on each paw.

7. Flatten a piece of sand, and use a shape cutter to make oval spots for the dog. Place spots randomly on the body and the tail. Press each spot gently to secure. Add a small coil of sand for the collar and cut out a heart shape tag using a shape cutter.

8. To make the bone, roll a short coil of sand and use a shape cutter to make two circles for each end of the bone. Press the heart cutter into the middle of the bone..

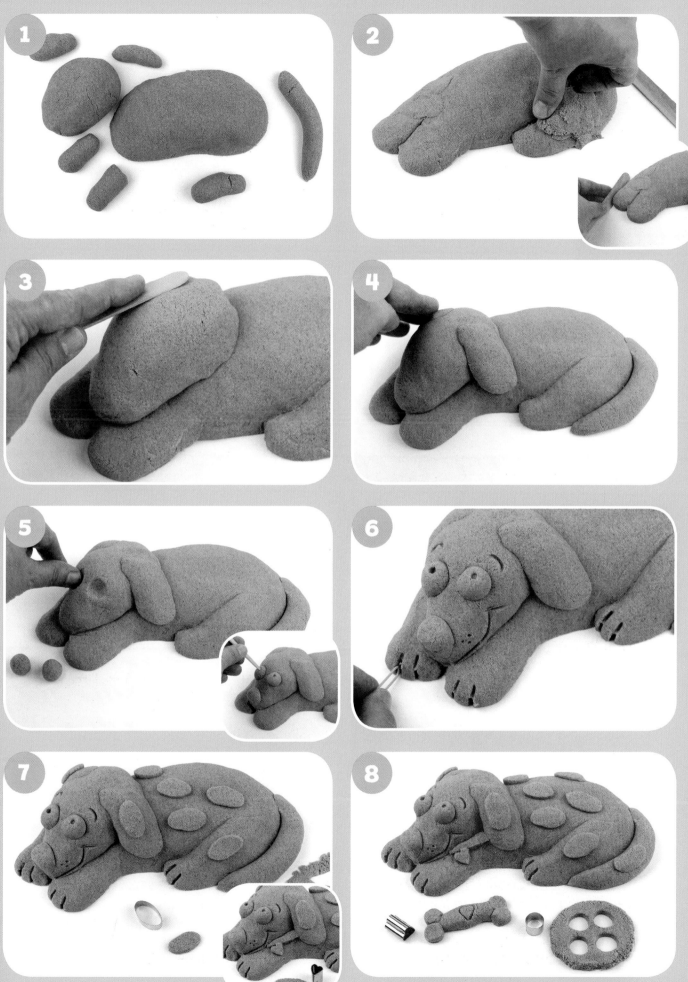

Cat & Mouse

Difficulty Level: ★ ★

Tools:
Shape Cutters
Paper clip
Fork
Sculpting tool
Craft stick

Directions:

1. Firmly pack an oval-shaped mound of sand for the body of the cat. Roll a large ball for the head, a medium size ball for the tail, and three smaller balls of sand for the feet.

2. Place the two front feet at one end of the body and press to attach. Add the head on top of the front feet. To make the back leg, roll the last ball of sand into a short thick coil and position next to the body. Use some loose sand to form the upper part of the back leg. Fill any cracks with loose sand and smooth out surface with your fingers and a craft stick.

3. Roll the sand for the tail into a tapered coil. Attach the larger end of the tail to the end of the cat and press the coil around the back leg of the cat.

4. Add two cones of sand to the top of the cat's head to form the ears. Use a craft stick to define the ears. Press the outside of each ear with your fingers while gently opening up the inside with a sculpting tool. The rounded end of the paper clip is used to make the cat's eyes, mouth, and eyebrows. Use the side of the paper clip to make the whiskers, and the open end of the paper clip to make the freckles.

5. The fork is used to add a furry texture to the cat. Gently pull the fork along the surface to create even lines. Don't add texture to the face; only the sides of the head. Pinch a triangle for the nose from the loose sand. Position on the face and press to attach.

6. To make the mouse, roll an egg-shaped ball of sand. Place a small amount of loose sand on the head. Pinch the sand to form the ears. Use a craft stick to define the shape.

7. Pack loose sand in a straw. Roll the straw in your fingers to release the coil. Use the coil to make a tail for the mouse. Pinch the end of the tail into a point.

8. Add details to the face using a paper clip.

Caterpillar

Difficulty Level: ★ ★

Tools:

Egg carton
Chopstick
Texture sheet
Paper clip

Directions:

1. Cut apart one section of an egg carton to use as a mold for the caterpillar. Pack the sand tightly into each cup and then turn the mold over to form the base of the body.

2. Use a texture sheet to round and add dotted texture to the body of the caterpillar.

3. While holding each end of the body, gently curve the form to give the caterpillar some character. If cracks appear in the sand, press gently with texture sheet to fill them in.

4. Roll ten short legs and place them at each section of the body. Roll a ball of sand and press it onto the end of the caterpillar to form the head.

5. Use your finger to make two indents for the eyes. Roll two eyeballs the same size.

6. Place the eyeballs in each indent.

7. Add a pupil to each eye by gently pressing the end of a chopstick into each eyeball.

8. To make a smile, press the rounded end of a paper clip into the sand.

Spot-O-Pillar!
Now that you have the basic caterpillar done, add some special details with sandy spots or shapes.

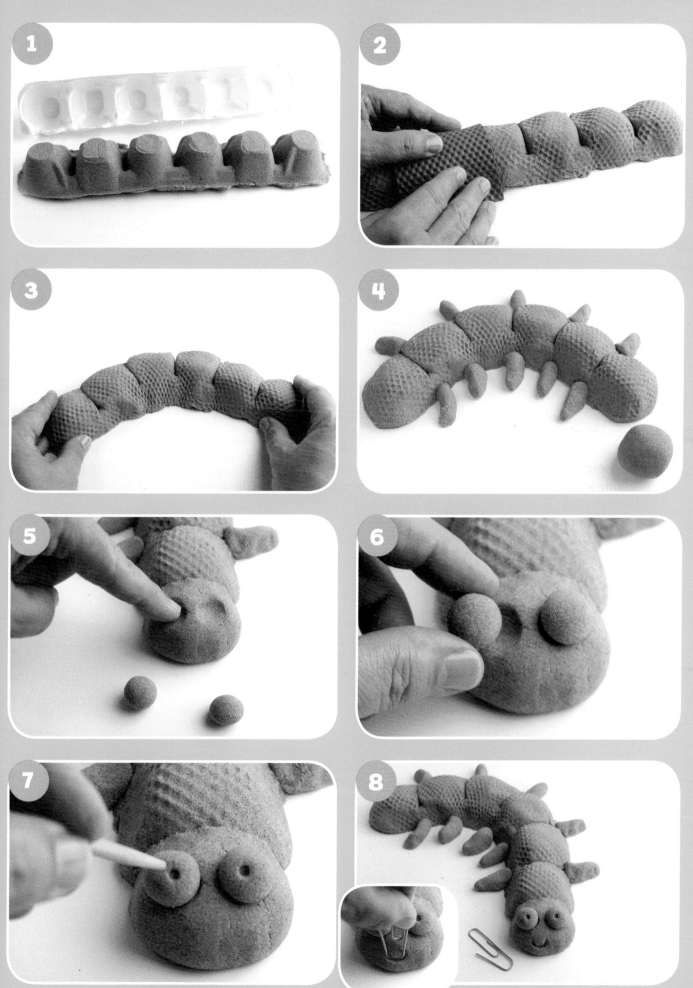

Monkey

Difficulty Level: ★ ★ ★

Tools:
Shape cutters
Craft stick
Texture sheet
Sculpting tool
Knife
Paper clip

Directions:

1. Firmly pack an oval-shaped mound of sand for the body and a smaller rounded mound of sand for the head. Roll two long thick coils of sand for the arms and legs. Make four equal size balls of sand for the hands and feet. Roll two balls of sand for the ears.

2. Cut the coils of sand into four equal length pieces. Position the body parts as shown. Flatten the hands and the feet, and cut out wedges of sand with the sculpting tool.

3. Round the fingers and toes using the sculpting tool, and position the hands and feet. Add a small mound of sand to form the belly.

4. Use a texture sheet to flatten the belly into place. The wavy texture sheet is used in this project. Use a craft stick to smooth the edge of the belly.

5. Add a half oval piece of flattened sand on the lower half of the face. Clean up edges with the craft stick.

6. Flatten a handful of sand and use a circle cutter to make a circle. Using a knife, slice off one piece of the circle to make a flat edge. Center it over the mouth piece and press gently into place. Fill in the join with loose sand and smooth with a craft stick.

7. Divide the eyebrows using a craft stick.

8. Cut two circles for the eyes using the shape cutters. Draw a mouth with the paper clip and use the paper clip to add details to the face.

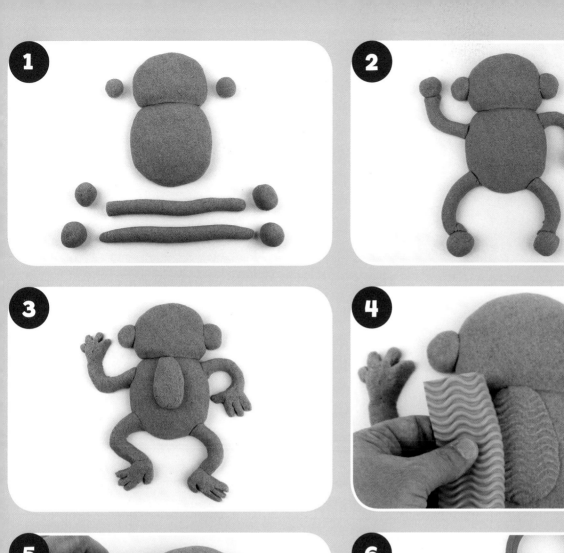

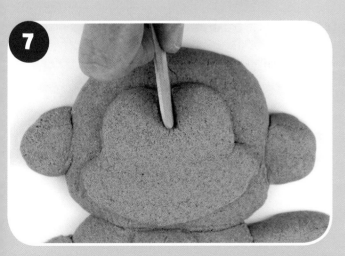

Turtle

Difficulty Level: ★ ★ ★

Tools:
Shape Cutters
Chopstick
Toothpick
Texture sheet
Paper clip

Directions:

1. Make a firmly packed mound of sand to form the shell of the turtle. Round out the top of it by pressing with your hand.

2. To create the head, roll a ball of sand and press it gently onto the turtle shell. Add four coils of sand for the legs and a cone shape for the tail.

3. Use a dotted texture sheet to pattern the shell, legs, head, and tail of the turtle.

4. Flatten sand and cut out five diamond shapes to decorate the turtle shell.

5. Cut seven circles out of the flattened sand.

6. Add diamond and circle shapes to the shell to create a pattern. Use the side of the paper clip to make lines on the shell, and divide the shell into sections. Add detail lines to the center of each diamond shape using the paperclip. Use the two remaining circles to make the eyes. Position the eyes on the head of the turtle and press gently to attach.

7. Use the rounded end of the paper clip to add an eyebrow over each eye. Use the side of the paper clip to add a mouth and two lines to the end of each foot.

8. Use a chopstick to make a pupil in each eye. Use the toothpick to add two nostril holes.

Shell Design!
Try a flower design for a different turtle look!

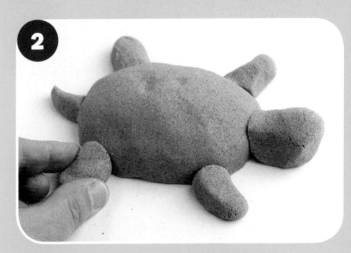

Dragon

Difficulty Level: ★ ★ ★

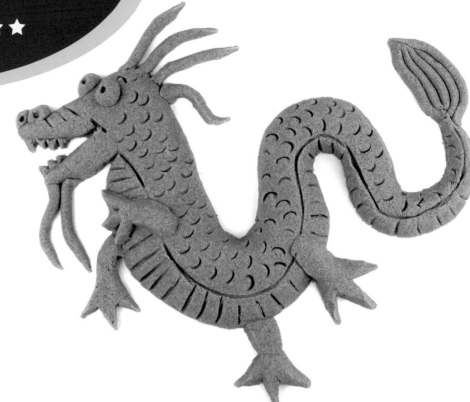

Tools:
Shape Cutters
Chopstick
Paper clip
Straw
Craft stick
Sculpting tool
Knife

Directions:

1. Firmly pack a long tapered coil for the body of the dragon. Roll an egg shape for the head.

2. Add the head to the thicker end of the body, and fill in any cracks with loose sand. Use the craft stick to smooth the surface and sides of the dragon. Use the knife to cut halfway through the head to form the mouth. Rock the knife back and forth to open the mouth.

3. To make the thin beard, tail, and head coils, use a drinking straw. Push the straw through loose sand and tap filled straw on the table to tightly pack the sand. Gently roll the straw through your fingers to release the coil.

4. Use the paper clip to add details to the body of the dragon. Start under the chin and draw a line down the entire length of the body. Add belly lines using the side of the paper clip. The rounded end of the paper clip is used to make the scale pattern. Use the paperclip to add ridges to the nose and a line for the mouth.

5. Use coils and balls of sand to make the legs and feet of the dragon. Cut two wedges out of each flattened ball to create the feet. Position legs and feet as shown.

6. Roll two balls of sand for the eyes and position them on head and press gently to attach. Add a pupil to each eye using the end of a chopstick.

7. Make two smaller balls of sand for the nostrils. Position nostrils on the end of the nose and press gently to attach. Add nostril holes using the chopstick.

8. Add a small coil of sand for the upper and lower teeth. Use the sculpting tool to form the pointed teeth.

Koi Pond

Difficulty Level: ★ ★ ★

Tools:

Shape Cutters
Chopstick
Paper clip
Fork
Knife
Craft stick

Directions:

1. Flatten a large amount of sand and use a fork to add water texture to the entire piece. You could also use a wavy texture sheet to form the water pattern.

2. Firmly pack a mound of sand for the body of the fish. Roll two cone-shaped pieces of sand for the tail and two smaller cones of sand for the fins. Roll a coil of sand to fit along the back of the fish.

3. Press all the pieces of the body, fins and tail into place. Smooth the edge of the fish carefully. Try not to mess up the pattern of the water. Add detail lines to the fins, tail, and back fin using a craft stick. Use a craft stick to add gill lines to the fish.

4. Use the rounded end of the paperclip to make a scale pattern.

5. Make two whiskers on each side of the head by piling up a thin line of sand and pinching it into a ridge to form the whisker. Make two indents with your thumb to hold the eyes.

6. Roll two oval-shaped eyes and place them in the indents. Add a pupil to each eye with the end of the chopstick. To form the mouth, use the chopstick to create an opening.

7. Add a pancake of sand for the water lily, and use the craft stick to smooth the surface of the leaf and add detail lines. Add a rock with a mound of sand and use your fingers or a craft stick to slightly smooth the surface. Add some flowers using the shape cutters to make the petals and the flower center from a flattened piece of sand.

8. Cut the edge of the pond with a knife in a wavy fashion to finish the koi pond.

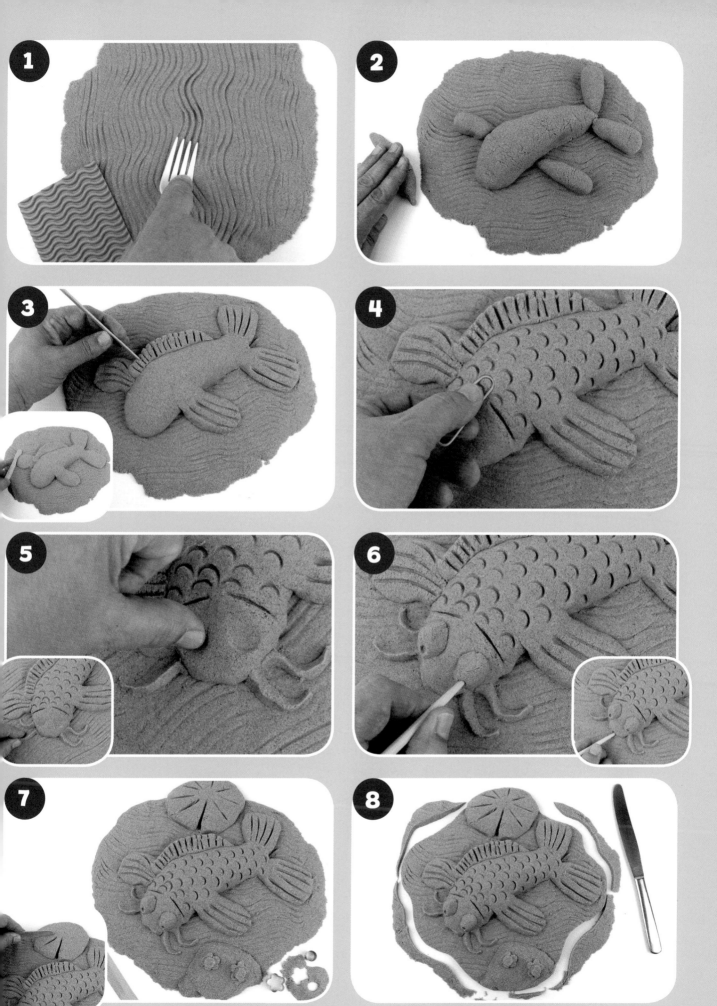

Peacock

Difficulty Level: ★ ★ ★

Tools:

Shape Cutters
Paper clip
Craft stick
Tape roller
Fork
Knife

Directions:

1. Make a half circle of flattened sand, use a knife and a craft stick to define the edge.

2. Use a fork to make a scored texture for the tail. Start the fork from the outside edge and draw into the center; repeat to fill the shape with the ribbed texture.

3. Firmly pack an oval of sand for the body of the peacock. Position it with about a third hanging over the bottom edge of the tail as shown. Add loose sand and smooth into the neck, head, and beak of the bird. Use the craft stick to refine the shape.

4. Add a cone shape for the wing and flatten onto the body of the peacock.

5. Use the craft stick to refine and smooth the top and edge of the wing.

6. Pack loose sand into the tape roller to form five disks of sand for the base of the tail. Place them on the peacock and press gently to attach.

7. Use the fork to add texture to the body of the peacock. The craft stick is used to add deeper detail lines to the tail and the long feathers on the end of the wing. To make the feather pattern, use the rounded end of the paper clip.

8. Pack loose sand into the tape roller to form seventeen disks of sand for tail feathers. Place nine in the arch closest to the body. Pinch one side of each disk to form a point. (Directions continued on page 46)

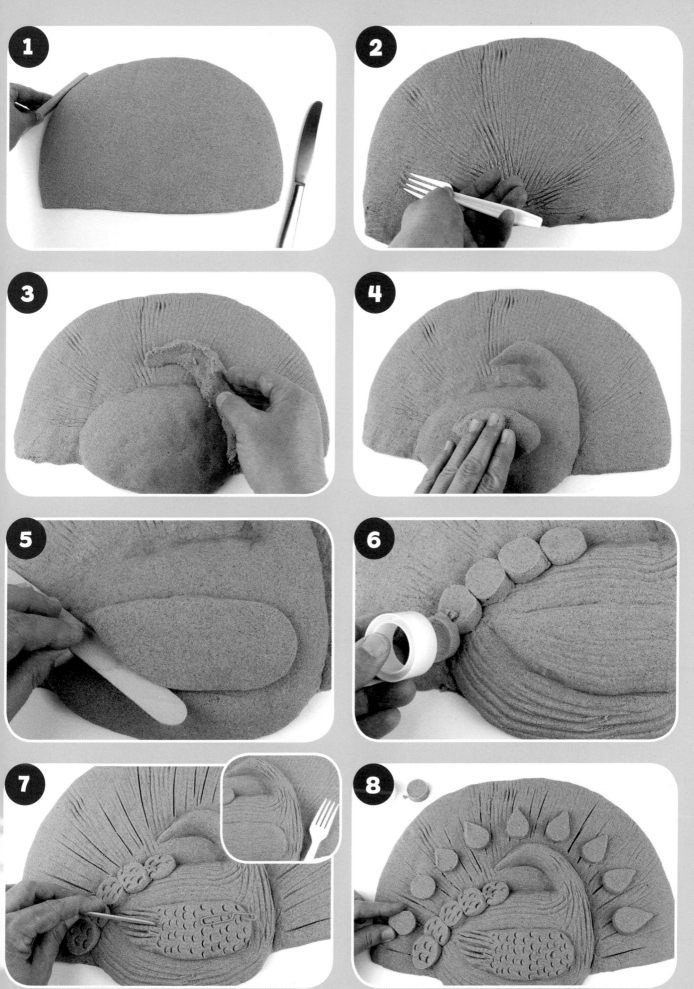

Peacock
Continued

Directions Continued:

9. Place the remaining eight disks of sand on the tail. Position the second row between each feather on the first row. Space the feathers evenly around the tail. Pinch each disk as you did in step 8. Use a leaf shape cutter to make an imprint in the middle of each of the feathers.

10. Use a circle cutter to cut out small rounds of sand and place one at the wide end of each feather.

11. Cut out a leaf shape piece of sand and place it on the head to form the eye. Add a circle of sand to make the eyeball. Use the point of a paper clip to make the pupil of the eye. Make a small line to define the beak and add two nostril holes with the end of the paper clip.

12. Use the side of the paper clip to add two lines to the top of each feather.

13. Flatten a piece of sand and cut a crown shape using the knife.

14. Add the crown to the head of the peacock.

15. Cut out the edge of the tail using the knife in a wave pattern, following the placement of the feathers.

16. Gently smooth around the cut edge.

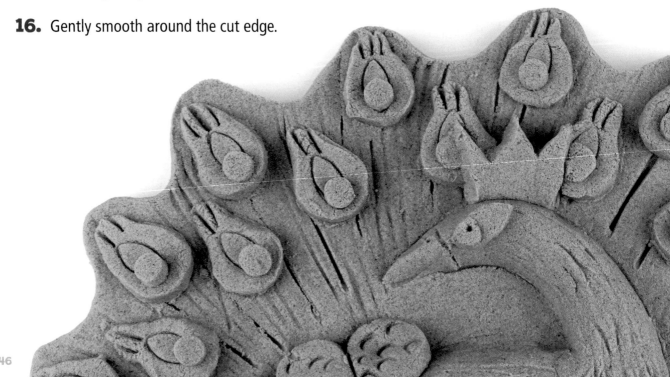

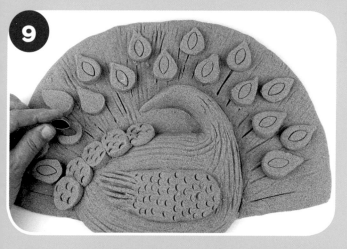

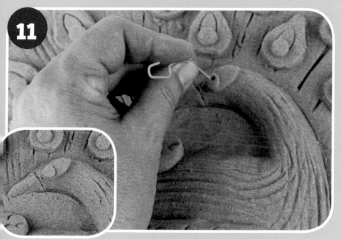

Jazz it up!